BOX OF TRICKS

presents

NARVIK

a new play with songs by

Lizzie Nunnery

NARVIK

Cast in order of appearance

JIM CALLAGHAN	Joe Shipman
ELSE DAHL/LUCYA	Nina Yndis
KENNY ATWOOD/	
SID CALLAGHAN	Lucas Smith
THE BAND	Vidar Norheim
	Maz O'Connor
	Joe Hirons

Director	Hannah Tyrrell-Pinder
Designer	Katie Scott
Associate Producer	Amy Fisher
Lighting Designer	Richard Owen
Composers	Vidar Norheim, Martin Heslop
Movement Director	Elinor Randle
Dramaturg	Lindsay Rodden
Production Manager	Richard Owen
Stage Manager	Stacy Armstrong

NARVIK received its world premiere in a production by
Box of Tricks Theatre Company at Liverpool Playhouse Studio
on 8 September 2015 with the following cast:

JIM CALLAGHAN	Joe Shipman
ELSE DAHL/LUCYA	Nina Yndis
KENNY ATWOOD/	
SID CALLAGHAN	Lucas Smith
THE BAND	Martin Heslop, Vidar Norheim, Lizzie Nunnery

Cast

JOE SHIPMAN | Jim Callaghan

Joe's theatre credits include: *Unsung* (Turflove and Dada Fest); *Narvik* (Box of Tricks Theatre Company); *The Maurie* (Writing on the Wall Festival); *Waiting for Brando* (national tour); *Alice Through the Winter Gardens* (Winter Gardens Blackpool); *Hatch* (Manchester 24/7); *Ten Tiny Toes*; *The Way Home* (Liverpool Everyman Theatre); *Slow Time* (20 Stories High); *Wrong Place, Right Time* (Contact Theatre); *Macbeth*, *The Trial* (Unity Theatre). Winner of Manchester 24/7 Festival Favourite Actor Award 2010 for performance in *Hatch*. Short film credits: *The Swimming Man* (LA Productions); *The Bowden Tapes*; *Unintended*. Radio credits: *The Big Toe Radio Show* (BBC 4); *Culture*; *Girl 2008*. Joe is also a founding member of street theatre collective Egg People for whom he performs at festivals nationally and internationally.

NINA YNDIS | Else Dahl/Lucya

Nina trained at the Royal Conservatoire of Scotland. Originally from Norway, she is London-based and is fluent in English, Norwegian and Polish. Stage credits include Else in *Narvik* at the Liverpool Playhouse Theatre, Lily Byrne in *A Man of No Importance*, Vivienne in *Legally Blonde* and Mrs Roach in *Betty Blue Eyes*. Screen credits include Kavetka in *Peaky Blinders*, Irena in the CBC series *X Company* and Jules in BBC 3's *5 by 5*. Working in the Norwegian film and TV industry Nina was seen in *Glassdukkene* directed by Nils Gaup. Earlier credits are the TV series *Spesialenheten* directed by Trond Berg-Nilssen.

LUCAS SMITH | Kenny Atwood/Sid Callaghan

Theatre credits: *Doctor Faustus* (Royal Exchange Theatre, Manchester); *Narvik* (Playhouse Theatre, Liverpool); *A Restless Place* (Theatre Royal, York; Pilot); *Last Train To Tomorrow*, *A Midsummer Night's Dream* (The Hallé, Manchester); *The Bombmaker*, *Icarus* (The Lowry, Salford Quays), *Measure For Measure*, *Icarus* (Edinburgh Fringe); *Beauty and The Beast*, *The Schoolmistress* (Stephen Joseph Theatre, Scarborough); *Boomtown Gals* (Peggy Productions, national tour). Television includes: *Fresh Meat* (Channel 4 / E4). Film includes: *27 Memory Lane* (Lupton Films). Radio includes: *Adventures of the Soul, Brief Lives, The Small House at Allington* (BBC Radio).

VIDAR NORHEIM | The Band and Composer

Vidar Norheim is a multi-instrumentalist, composer and producer originally from Norway. He studied BA Music at LIPA where he now is a visiting lecturer. Vidar has toured worldwide as a member of Liverpool's alt pop unit Wave Machines, and worked extensively in a folk duo with Lizzie Nunnery. In 2011 he was named as Norway's most promising songwriting talent, winning a place at Song:Expo in Trondheim alongside many of the world's leading songwriters and producers. His solo debut EP entitled 'Blind Carbon Copy' was released in 2016, with further releases planned on labels in Japan, Norway and the UK.

His theatre credits as composer and sound designer include: *Narvik* (Box of Tricks, Liverpool Playhouse), *Cheer Up*, *This is Only the Beginning* (Liverpool Playhouse), *100 Seel Street* (site-specific), *Cartographers* (Theatre by the Lake) and *Pages from My Songbook* (Royal Exchange Theatre). In autumn 2014 he performed in *Bright Phoenix* in the Liverpool Everyman, a play by Jeff Young with music by Martin Heslop. Vidar has worked on projects with Willy Russell, Tim Firth and Frank Cottrell Boyce. Radio and TV composition credits include *The Singer*, an afternoon play for BBC Radio 4, and *Monkey Love*, a Three Minute Wonder for Channel 4. He is currently writing his first film score for the feature film *A World After*.

MAZ O'CONNOR | The Band

Maz O'Connor is a singer and songwriter. She has released two albums, *This Willowed Light* (2014) and *The Longing Kind* (2016), and toured the UK, Europe and Canada solo and with her band. She was a BBC Performing Arts Fund Fellow in 2013 and 2015. Previous theatre work includes a season at the RSC singing in *As You Like It* with music written by Laura Marling, and composing for an RSC celebration event at 10 Downing Street in June 2015.

JOE HIRONS | The Band

Joe is a versatile multi-instrumentalist musician, composer and performer. He trained as a musical director and composer as part of the Hope Street Ltd Emerging Artist Programme in Liverpool in 2012 and went on to write and record music for a number of projects that were performed as part of Threshold Festival and On the Verge Festival in 2013. Joe has worked as a composer and performer with Petite Ullaloom Theatre Company, and in the last two years, has toured nationally with Travelled Companions Theatre Company.

Creative Team

LIZZIE NUNNERY | Playwright

Lizzie's first theatre play *Intemperance* (Liverpool Everyman, Sept 2007) was awarded 5 stars by The Guardian and shortlisted for the Meyer-Whitworth Award. She was one of the writers of the critically acclaimed *Unprotected* which was awarded the Amnesty International Award for Freedom of Expression (Liverpool Everyman, Traverse Edinburgh 2006). Lizzie's full-length play *The Swallowing Dark* was shortlisted for the Susan Smith Blackburn Award and reopened the Liverpool Playhouse Studio in October 2011, with a subsequent run at Theatre503 in London. In September 2015 her play with songs *Narvik* was produced by Box of Tricks with a two-week run in the Liverpool Playhouse Studio, and a national tour January–March 2017. She has worked with Druid, Slung Low, the Gate, Trestle, Paines Plough and Cardboard Citizens. Current commissions include the Liverpool Everyman, the Royal Exchange Manchester and the National Theatre. She has written extensively for BBC Radio and her latest radio series *The Hanleys* was broadcast on Radio 4 in December 2016. Lizzie's debut short film *Monkey Love* aired in 2009 on Channel 4. In the same year she researched and developed a pitch for a children's drama series with Lime Pictures as part of a writing team led by Frank Cottrell Boyce. In February 2013 she won *Little Brother's Big Opportunity* and is currently developing original TV ideas with Little Brother Productions. She is also a singer and songwriter, performing regularly with producer/composer Vidar Norheim. Releases include albums *Company of Ghosts* (Fellside Recordings 2010) and *Black Hound Howling* (Red Thread 2012). Their latest EP *Songs of Drink and Revolution* was released in 2013 to critical acclaim.

HANNAH TYRRELL-PINDER | Director

Hannah trained as a director at Mountview Academy of Theatre Arts and is Joint Artistic Director of Box of Tricks. Directing credits for Box of Tricks include: *Narvik* (Liverpool Playhouse Studio); *In Doggerland* (national tour); *Word:Play/NWxSW* (Regional Tour); *Picture a City* (Everyword 2012, Liverpool Playhouse); *London Tales* (Waterloo East and Nu:Write Festival, Zagreb); *Head/Heart* (national tour); *Word:Play 4* (Arcola); *True Love Waits* (Latitude, Pulse, Nu:Write Festivals); *Word:Play 3* (Theatre503); *Whispering Happiness* (Tristan Bates); *Captain of the School Football Team* (Hotbed and Latitude festivals, 2009); *Word:Play 2* (Theatre503); *Word:Play* (Union Theatre); *A Hole in the Fence* and *Rural* (White Bear). Other directing includes: *Night of the Soul* (ALRA North), *Uprising* (Monkeywood at The Lowry), *JB Shorts 11* (Joshua Brooks), *Narvik* (Everyword 2013), *100 Seel St* (The Alligator Club, Liverpool), *JB Shorts 7* (Joshua Brooks). She is a freelance workshop leader for the Actors' Guild and the Actors' Lab, a script reader for the Royal Exchange and the Bruntwood Playwriting Prize and co-founder of Direct North, a network for emerging theatremakers in the North West.

AMY FISHER | Associate Producer

Amy is a producer from the North West. She was the recipient of a BBC Performing Arts Fellowship in 2014 – one of the '32 to watch' – working with Box of Tricks as an Associate Producer. Producing credits include *Plastic Figurines* (Box of Tricks national tour), *Narvik* (Box of Tricks in association with Liverpool Everyman & Playhouse), *Chip Shop Chips* (Box of Tricks rural tour), *River Lane* (Eastern Angles Theatre Company). Amy also works as Community Projects Producer at Theatre Royal Plymouth. Credits include *18* (Theatre Royal Plymouth), *Short Changed* (Theatre Royal Plymouth) and *We're Here because We're Here* (National Theatre and Theatre Royal Plymouth).

KATIE SCOTT | Designer

Katie is an award-winning designer based in the North West. After graduating from LIPA in 2012, Katie was the inaugural recipient of the Liverpool Everyman & Playhouse Prize for Theatre Design. Credits for Box of Tricks include: *Plastic Figurines* (Box of Tricks national tour), *Chip Shop Chips* (Box of Tricks Northern tour). Other credits Include: *Held* (Liverpool Playhouse Studio – winner of Liverpool Daily Post Arts Award for Best Design 2012), *We Are the Multitude* (24:7 Festival – MTA nominee Best Fringe Show), *Gargantua* (NT Connections, Lowry Young Company), *The Ballad of Rudy* (Goblin Theatre, Royal Exchange Studio), *The Grid* (Young Everyman Playhouse Company), *Dark Dark Wood* (Unity Theatre, Liverpool).

RICHARD OWEN | Lighting Designer and Production Manager

Most recently: *Hansel and Gretel* (Horse and Bamboo), *Witness* (Kate Jackson at Tatton Park), *Plastic Figurines* (Box of Tricks at NDT), *Flexn Iceland* (MIF and Reykjavik Arts Festival), *Country Wife* (MMU at HOME), *Narvik* (Box of Tricks at Liverpool Playhouse Studio), *Edmund the Learned Pig* (Fitting Multimedia), *Flexn* (MIF), *Plastic Figurines* (Box of Tricks national tour), *Rolling Stone* (Royal Exchange Theatre and West Yorkshire Playhouse), *Manpower* (2Destination Language) and *Tree* (Daniel Kitson at The Old Vic, London).

Past designs include: for Royal Exchange Theatre, *The Gatekeeper*, *Winter-Long*, *Powder Monkey*, *Salt*, *The Palace of the End*, *Dr Korzack's Example*, *Jonah and Otto*, *The Flags*, *Monster*, *Christmas is Miles Away*, *Come Blow Your Horn*, *Mayhem*, *The Rise and Fall of Little Voice*, *The Happiest Days of Your Life*, *Rafts and Dreams*, *Across Oka*, *Dead Wait*, *On My Birthday*; for Crucible Theatre Sheffield, *Brassed Off*, *Bouncers*, *Educating Rita*, *Bedevilled* and *The Little Mermaid*; for Horse and Bamboo Theatre Company, *In the Shadow of Trees* and *Veil*.

MARTIN HESLOP | Composer

Martin Heslop is a composer and writer. His work for theatre has included writing songs, poems and music for *Bright Phoenix* (Liverpool Everyman Theatre), *Cartographers* (Theatre by the Lake, Keswick), *Radical City*

(Liverpool Everyman) and *Stories in the Walls* (UnConvention Tyneside). He has also written for site-specific shows in places such as a thirteenth-century tower in Newcastle's city walls, Chester Castle and St Georges Hall. His theatre work as a sound designer includes *Scarberia* (York Theatre Royal). He recently composed the soundtrack to *Spider-Web City*, a short film which premiered at Uncharted Festival, Albania. Martin has collaborated across art forms as a writer, poet, composer and musician, for performance, publications and installations. He has recently had a collection of poems, *Body*, published by Dock Road Press.

ELINOR RANDLE | Movement Director

Elinor is Artistic Director of Tmesis Theatre, acclaimed UK-based physical theatre company, and Physical Fest (Liverpool's International Physical Theatre Festival). Elinor has performed in or directed, all of Tmesis Theatre's past productions, touring nationally and internationally for the past twelve years. She has collaborated with world-renowned practitioners on the pieces, including Tanya Khabarova (Derevo), Nigel Charnock, Lorna Marshall and Malou Airaudo (Pina Bausch Tanztheater). Tmesis Theatre has received critical acclaim for its dynamic physical theatre and recently won the award for 'Best Choreography at the United Solo Theatre Festival, New York 2015. Elinor also works as a lecturer at LIPA (Liverpool Institute for Performing Arts), is a trained yoga teacher and has worked as a movement director for many companies nationally, including 20 Stories High, Box of Tricks, Peepolykus and the Everyman and Playhouse.

                    www.tmesistheatre.com   www.physicalfest.com

LINDSAY RODDEN | Dramaturg

Lindsay Rodden is a writer and dramaturg. Lindsay's writing for theatre includes *Cartographers* (Theatre by the Lake); work with women playwrights' collective Agent 160 including *A Modest Proposal* (Theatre503, The Arches and Chapter Arts Centre) and *Sunday Morning*, *Dandelion Seeds* (Wales Millennium Centre); verbatim play *Ends* (Liverpool Everyman, tour); *Man with Bicycle*, *'73* and *Writing in the Dark* (The Miniaturists) and *The Almond Tree* (State of Wonder). She is currently writing an adaptation of Brian Patten's *The Story Giant* for the Liverpool Everyman, Spring 2017. She is also writer in residence at Northumbria University and Live Theatre, Newcastle. Lindsay was invited to join the Royal Court's inaugural National Writers' Group, and Dublin International Theatre Festival's prestigious artists' programme The Next Stage. For some years Lindsay was Literary Associate for Liverpool Everyman & Playhouse, running new writing festival Everyword, and the dramaturg on many of the theatres' productions, including *Bright Phoenix* and *Hope Place* (Everyman), *Scrappers* and *Held* (Playhouse Studio). She has worked as a dramaturg in both Ireland and the UK, most recently on *Narvik* (Box of Tricks, touring 2017).

The new play makers

'A theatre company to watch'
The Stage

**Celebrating a decade of new play making this year,
Box of Tricks is a Manchester-based theatre company
that champions the next generation of playwrights,
producing top quality new plays on local and national stages.**

We are a launchpad for new talent. We commission and develop
bold and original new plays from the most exciting new voices,
creating ambitious and heartfelt theatre that engages, challenges
and entertains. We stage new plays in Manchester and the North
and tour productions to audiences nationwide.

We are the next generation. We are the new play makers.
We are Box of Tricks.

Recent productions include: *Plastic Figurines* by Ella Carmen Greenhill
(New Diorama and national tour), *Chip Shop Chips* by Becky Prestwich
(Northern tour), *Narvik* by Lizzie Nunnery (Liverpool Playhouse Studio),
In Doggerland by Tom Morton-Smith (national tour).

www.boxoftrickstheatre.co.uk

Thank you to

Our Playmaker Patrons (Sue Tyrrell, John and Gloria Quayle, Ed Benson and
Kath Quick); Matthew Linley and The Unity Theatre, Liverpool; Ben Lloyd,
Victoria Rope and everyone at the Liverpool Everyman and Playhouse;
Kellie Hotten, Kate Kordel and Stephen Fletcher for the development
of the play; LIPA; The Royal Exchange Theatre; Jonathan Hunter;
our Board (Caz Brader, Chris Honer, Andrew Pinder, John Quayle).

Developed with support from the Liverpool Everyman & Playhouse
e&P Talent Fund.

Production supported by the Unity Theatre, Liverpool.

Supported by

and The Leche Trust

Narvik

Lizzie Nunnery's first play, *Intemperance* (Liverpool Everyman, 2007), was awarded five stars by the *Guardian* and shortlisted for the Meyer-Whitworth Award. She co-wrote *Unprotected*, awarded the Amnesty International Award for Freedom of Expression (Everyman/Traverse, Edinburgh, 2006). *The Swallowing Dark* (Liverpool Playhouse Studio/Theatre503, 2011) was shortlisted for the Susan Smith Blackburn Award. *Narvik* (Box of Tricks/Playhouse Studio, 2015) is touring nationally January–March 2017. Forthcoming work includes *The People Are Singing* (Manchester Royal Exchange Studio, April 2017), a play with songs, *The Sum* (Everyman, May–June, 2017) and *Horny Handed Tons of Soil* (Unity Theatre, Liverpool, July 2017). She has written extensively for BBC Radio and is also a singer and songwriter, performing regularly with producer/composer Vidar Norheim.

LIZZIE NUNNERY

Narvik

a play with songs

FABER & FABER

First published in 2017
by Faber and Faber Limited
74–77 Great Russell Street, London WC1B 3DA

Typeset by Country Setting, Kingsdown, Kent CT14 8ES
Printed in England by CPI Group (UK) Ltd, Croydon CR0 4YY

A CIP record for this book is available from the British Library

ISBN 978-0-571-33741-5

2 4 6 8 10 9 7 5 3

For my grandfather Bill Mothershaw
who loved poetry

With thanks to
Lindsay Rodden, Victoria Rope,
Gemma Bodinetz, Matthew Linley,
Hannah Tyrrell Pinder
and all at Box of Tricks Theatre

Narvik opened at HOME, Manchester, on 31 January 2017, at the start of a national tour. The cast was as follows:

Jim Callaghan Joe Shipman
Else Dahl / Lucya Nina Yndis
Kenny Atwood / Sid Callaghan Lucas Smith
The Band Vidar Norheim, Maz O'Connor, Joe Hirons

Director Hannah Tyrrell-Pinder
Designer Katie Scott
Associate Producer Amy Fisher
Lighting Designer Richard Owen
Composers Vidar Norheim and Martin Heslop
Movement Director Elinor Randle
Dramaturg Lindsay Rodden
Production Manager Richard Owen
Stage Manager Stacy Armstrong

Narvik received its world premiere in a production by Box of Tricks Theatre Company at Liverpool Playhouse Studio on 8 September 2015 with the following cast:

Jim Callaghan Joe Shipman
Else Dahl / Lucya Nina Yndis
Kenny Atwood / Sid Callaghan Lucas Smith
The Band Martin Heslop, Vidar Norheim, Lizzie Nunnery

Characters

Jim Callaghan
ninety/early twenties, from Liverpool

Else Dahl
twenty-five, from Oslo

Lucya
thirties, Russian

Kenny Atwood
thirties, from London

Sid Callaghan
mid-twenties/early forties, Jim's father

The Band
three musicians
piano, harmonium, mandolin,
percussion, synth, voice

Else and Lucya are played by one actor
Kenny and Sid are played by one actor

Notes
The members of the band represent the dead
watching Jim, judging him

A dash (–) at the end of a line indicates an interruption

An ellipsis (. . .) indicates a search for a thought or words

Songs

'Where's Your Love?'
Scene Two, Scene Six, Scene Fourteen

'Boys We'll Rise'
Scene Five

'Echo Song'
Scene Three, Scene Seven, Scene Ten

'The Fox'
Scene Six

'Da blühen keine Rosen'
Scene Three, Scene Nine

'Katjuscha'
Scene Twelve

'Take My Heart'
Scene Twelve

Lyrics and poems are original apart from
'The Fox' (anonymous), 'Suk/A Sigh' by Bjørnson,
'Da blühen keine Rosen' (traditional),
'Katjuscha' (traditional)

NARVIK

The Set

Scattered or hanging from the ceiling are old tools,
torn metal, pipes, buckets, a radio, a Morse code
transmitter etc. Instruments the band play are also
scattered about. This is a basement, a ship, an
attic room, the coast of Norway, the Arctic . . .
Water is on the ground

SCENE ONE: THE FALL

Darkness. Faint high-pitched ringing. Jim, an old man, lies on the floor. He clutches a wet rag.

Jim I reach for it . . . find it by memory – fingers along the damp brick, cold soaking through my slippers. I reach, reach again and it happens so quickly. My hand misses the pipe and my hand misses the wall and my body reels forward then back so I'm flung loose and then the thud of my torso on the ground, the crack of my skull on the concrete.

A glimmer of light falls on Jim.

And the singing silence after. The knowledge of it. The wet, sinking knowledge – stupid bastard that I am. Stupid, stupid –

Else Jim?

The sound of rushing water fades up, loud and dangerous.

Jim And if I could've got hold of it – got something round it – if I could've stopped up the flow –

Else Come here, Jim.

Jim If the ground hadn't been wet, if I could've been steadier, if I hadn't slipped back. If I hadn't gone reeling . . . If I can't fix a broken pipe in my own bleeding house . . .

He struggles to get up, pushing against the floor and falling back again, again. He isn't strong enough. Sound of rushing water continues. He puts his hand to the back of his head – it's bleeding.

Jim How much cold?

Else I can't see you.

Jim How much will it take?

Else Come here.

Jim How much cold and how much blood?

Else, Kenny and the Band move towards him. The Band and Kenny are dressed in naval uniforms, Else in a long dress. All are pale, grey, as if seen beneath water. Jim struggles and fails again to get up, his movements growing smaller and weaker.

Else Let me see you.

Jim How much cold and how much blood and how much time? The snow banking up on the basement windows . . . No one to see me so old. So old and so useless to myself.

Else Jim?

Jim I'm here. (*Beat.*) I'm here.

Else / The Band (*sung*)
Where'd your love go lonely one
He sleeps beneath the waves
Where's your love, your only one
Where fishes move, where darkness waits
Full fathom five, oh vow and sigh
You'll search the seas below
But where your love's gone, lonely one
No living soul can go.

SCENE TWO: OSLO, APRIL 1939

The edge of the city, the edge of the Oslo fjord. A wooden quayside. Else approaches the water quickly, looking behind. She dances and sways, jumps between planks, slightly drunk.

Else (*sung*)
    Where's your love, your only son?
    He sleeps beneath the waves.
    Where's your love, your only one?
    His shining coat, his cap his gun.

    Young Jim approaches and watches. He's also been drinking.

Jim Thought I'd lost you then.

Else Come here, let me see you.

Jim (*looking up*) Jesus, look at that.

Else The sky?

Jim They're like knives.

Else You followed me here to see the view?

Jim It's not a bad one. Better than the Mersey. Mersey's alright like.

Else Water is water.

Jim You're serious?

Else I'm full of drink. Come over here.

Jim Vikings sailed out of here, you know?

Else Is that so?

Jim They had maps – all wrong. Stars and stories, half made-up. I read a book on it.

Else A whole book?

Jim Imagine sailing out with no idea when you'd hit land. No idea what was underneath. Mermaids and sea monsters. Like putting your hands out in the dark.

Else I hate the sea.

Jim You what?

Else Put me in the water, I scream and scream.

Jim An Oslo girl afraid of water?

Else I'm a schoolteacher. What do I have to do with the water?

Jim You're a *teacher*?

Else A history teacher. But thank you for your lesson on the Vikings.

Jim Shit.

Else This book you read: I'm not sure it was a good one.

Jim Well, it was more of a . . . comic. (*Beat.*) Cartoons and that . . .

She grins at him. He grins back.

Else Let me see you.

Jim It's a shame, you know?

Else What is?

Jim The water. You don't know what you're missing.

Else I know just what. When I was very young a boy pushed me in this fjord. Underwater with my coat and mittens filling up. I think you've never felt cold like that.

Jim Once or twice. You give it a minute – it warms up.

Else The big brave man.

Jim You move around, it starts to move with you. You get the rhythm and the swell gets under you . . . You get light. You forget yourself.

Else What do you want to forget?

Jim shrugs.

Jim Don't you ever want to slip out of your skin?

Else Definitely.

She holds his eye a moment.

Jim Shut your eyes.

Else Why? What will you do?

Jim Shut your eyes.

Else Do I know you so well?

Jim Shut your eyes and think of all the endless water, all the endless ways to go.

Else (*closing her eyes, shuddering*) All that darkness and silence.

Jim I could turn on a radio now and we'd hear fishing boats and cargo ships and cruisers halfway into the Atlantic, all talking to each other . . . radio signals zipping from New York to Toronto to Timbuktu. There's no dark and silence out there. It's all lit up.

Else (*opening her eyes*) Give me America. Wide lands. Dry heat. Yellow sun.

Jim You haven't got it so bad.

Else The great grey city and the great grey ocean.

Jim How you gonna get to America if you don't go on a ship?

Else Ships are fine. That I can do. You can take me on your ship: show me California and Virginia.

Jim My ship's a fishing boat.

Else So I'll sleep with the haddock and the cod.

Jim You're a loony.

Else Why don't you come over here?

Jim I saw you dancing back there, I thought, 'She looks like a nice sensible girl'.

Else I can't see your face.

Jim But no, you're a raving loony.

Else Are you afraid?

Jim What?

Else Inside you weren't afraid. Dancing with all the girls.

Jim What's to be afraid of?

Else Maybe it's only the dancing you like. All posture and no . . . what do you say? Substance.

Beat. He approaches her. She kisses him briefly.

Else (*pronouncing it 'Yim'*) Jim . . .

Jim (*correcting*) Jim.

Else *Jim*. I like it.

Jim I like you.

Else If I was you I'd have so much fun. I'd have girls in Liverpool and New York and Toronto and every Norsk port.

Jim I've had girls. They weren't like you.

Else I'm flattered.

Jim I never met an Elsie.

Else (*correcting his pronunciation*) Else.

Jim (*copying*) Else. Else . . . Else.

Else Say it three times and I'll disappear.

    The Band whispers with Jim as he repeats her name.

Jim Else. Else. Else.

SCENE THREE: GHOSTS

The Band play sounds of the basement: shimmering, wet and metallic. These sounds gradually form a loose rhythm. Rushing water can still be heard. Jim is lying on the floor and lit as in Scene One. He's delirious. Kenny sits on a chair nearby, smoking. He's in shadow, his cigarette glowing.

Kenny There he is . . . Jimmy the Mouth.

Jim If I can reach. If I can grip . . . If I can get a nail's hold, if I can get an elbow up, if I can get my arms to bear down and push off –

Kenny What's it gonna *be*, Jim?

Jim If I can get my stomach to hold firm so I can lift, so I can sit. If I can get my back to tense, my shoulders to roll –

Kenny You and your talk.

Jim If I can sit I can lean, if I can lean I can crouch, if I can crouch I can crawl. And then . . . and then –

Kenny You and your talk and nothing else.

Jim I can't see, Kenny. It's all broken up . . . There's something there . . .

Kenny Move.

Jim Something about bones, something about the stars and moonlight –

Kenny *Move, Jim.*

Jim I *can't move.*

Kenny That's the fucking rot.

Jim I'm ninety years old and there's nothing left in me, so you tell *me* what it's gonna *be.*

Kenny lights a match: his face visible while the match burns. They look at each other.

Kenny It'll be quick, I reckon. When it gets going.

Jim You think so?

Kenny It'll seem quick when you're in it.

Jim Like slipping over the edge of the world.

Kenny You won't even be thinking.

Jim What if I start thinking?

Kenny What if you start writing a bloody poem?

Jim laughs.

Jim
The fox and his wife they had a great strife,
They'd never eat mustard in all their life;
They'd eat their meat without fork or knife,
And lov'd to be picking a bone ee-oh.

The fox jump'd up on a moonlight night;
The stars they were shining and all things bright . . .

He searches for the rest, blinking.

The stars they were shining and all things bright . . .

Come on, what's next?

Kenny There's nothing in that. Nothing good.

Jim Come on, I always used to do this one.

Kenny (*retreating*) I mean it, Jimmy – no fucking poetry.

Jim Sing then. For morale. Please –

Kenny Any bastard can sing, Jim.

Jim For me, Ken.

Kenny (*sung*)
  Auf einem Seemannsgrab,
  Da blühen keine Rosen . . .

Jim Stop it. Stop it: that's not funny.

Kenny (*sung*)
  Auf einem Seemannsgrab,
  Da blüht kein Blümelein . . .

Jim (*reaching for Kenny*) Help me.

Kenny (*sung*) Der einz'ge Gruß . . .

Jim Help me why don't you?

Kenny You and your talk and nothing else.

Jim Help me, Kenny.

Kenny You'll talk the ocean dry.

Jim Help me or leave me.

Kenny It'll be freezing. Mark my words. Icicle time.

Jim Did you freeze, Kenny, or did you burn?

Kenny It's not the cold you'll be worried about.

Jim Nothing worries me, mate. I'm iron. I'm *stone*.

Kenny There'll be nothing *to you*, Jim.

Kenny flicks his cigarette on to Jim and moves away into shadow. Jim twists helpless on the floor, reaching out for him, panicking, gasping. Sid approaches softly, dimly lit.

Sid It's alright, kid. It's alright –

Jim tries to swivel round to see him.

It's only a story, Jimmy.

Jim I can't breathe, Dad.

Sid Don't panic – you'll make it worse.

Jim struggles again, trying to pull himself up, shaking with cold.

You hear me, Jimmy?

Jim If I could reach the wall . . . If I can reach I can sit. If I can sit I can kneel.

Sid Calm now. Stop now.

Jim If I can kneel I can crawl. If I can –

Sid (*sung, comforting*)
If my hands were not stone
And my feet not wood
And my body not bound
To the earth by blood
I'd cut through the air
Like a murder of crows . . .

Jim Your tune . . . I'd be in bed with asthma and you'd sing . . . Tell stories and poems. Chalk mountains and oceans on the walls. And the fox –

Sid The fox and his wife they had great strife

Jim Sharp little face . . . little grin. I always liked him best. Even though he was a bad fox. Maybe that's why I liked him.

Sid Sleep now.

Jim Tell me 'bout the ships, 'bout the war.

Sid It's too late, Jimmy.

Jim 'Bout the mermaids, the monsters –

Sid Go to sleep now.

Jim Again though. Tell me.

Sid Sleep now, Jimmy.

With a sudden surge of effort Jim fights to get up, rising and falling again and again, crying out in pain. He lies gasping. Lights shift.

SCENE FOUR: LETTERS

Oslo, July 1939.

Else leans back in a chair, looking out, holding a glass of gin with ice, humming. Slowly Jim rises and moves towards her, watching.

Else 'I can't sleep. The rain on the roof, on and on . . .'

Jim 'I can't sleep for thinking about you.'

Else 'Days and nights of rain in June. Everything's wet and shining – morning to evening.'

Jim 'I see you. I think about you and see you walking: sunlit through rain.'

Else 'Paraply. What do you call it? To cover my head?'

Jim 'I see you walking to the school in the bright white morning: an umbrella over your head. You walk from the centre to the tram and then watch the city go by for a mile, two miles.'

Else 'Rain and rain and the night is hot and long. The taste of gin reminds me of you.'

Jim 'At night your attic room is a star glinting above Oslo.'

Else 'Half the year in here I'm freezing. And now it seems I'm melting.'

Jim 'I see you sitting alone writing these letters.'

Else 'Tell me about where you are. Tell me what you do there.'

Jim 'I think of you out with your friends, at dances – with your hands in other men's hands . . .'

Else 'Don't tell me about the docks and the river. Tell me everything I don't already know.'

Jim 'I swam forty lengths in Cornwallis Street baths, salt water up my nose, and thought of you. Because you hate the sea but you smell like the sea, you smell like the salt and the air.'

Else 'Paraply. Sol. Regn.'

Jim 'How do you say it? Write it down for me.'

Else 'You ask such silly questions. They can't be the right questions.'

Jim 'I went up the social for the Sunday-night band, but I didn't dance with any of the girls.'

Else 'What is *the social* and why do you go *up* to it? This can't be good English.'

Jim 'And they asked me. You can bet I got offers. I turned them down flat.'

Else 'I've seen you dance – it's maybe for the best.'

Jim 'Or I danced with a few of them – but I didn't kiss them.'

Else ' "Elske. Jeg elske deg." That's "I love you." Why do you ask?'

Jim 'And I nearly got in a fight over you. Robbie Mac got hold of one of your letters – ran off down the dock with it – pages flying.'

Else 'Kjaereste. Min kjæreste. My dearest. That's another way to say it.'

Jim 'All the lads were laughing at me. Saying I had a sweetheart.'

Else 'Skatten min. My treasure. You can say it like that.'

Jim 'Well, I do have – I told them.'

Else 'My mother won't speak to me. My landlady told her I was playing around with a sailor.'

Jim 'If I can call you that. If that's what you'd call it.'

Else 'I asked her, "What's wrong with a little playing around?" She nearly fell down dead.'

Jim 'I told them: "Few more weeks you'll be laughing on your own. I'll be away and getting ready for fighting, not fishing." '

Else 'Am I playing around, Jim?'

Jim 'I had a dream about you. I was teaching you to swim and you started kicking and gasping – you were going under, but I caught you, I kept hold.'

Else 'Tell me about the radio signals. Tell me about the ships lit up. Tell me how everything's connected and nobody's alone.'

Jim 'Are you alone, Else? Is someone with you?'

Else 'There are things I'd say if I knew how. Maybe I can't say them in English. Maybe not in Norsk or any language.'

Jim 'I see all the places we'll go. I think about all the ways we'll travel.'

Else 'You told me you want to slip out of your skin. I think about that. I say those words again and again.'

Jim 'Liverpool and Oslo and the sea between. And the Arctic . . . the frozen ocean. And Archangel and Murmansk. Toronto and New York and California. And for each place: a different note. Each a different light in the dark.'

Else 'Come and see me, Jim.'

The Band move closer to him, humming, playing a gentle theme. As the music fades, Jim and Else find each other in the middle of the space. They hold on to each other.

Are you crying?

Jim No. You know I'm not.

She touches his face.

No one touches you on the ships. Weeks on end – no one comes near you if it's not a shove in the shoulder or a clip round the head and sometimes you're even glad of that.

Else I don't mind you crying –

Jim I'm *not* crying.

Else (*tracing his shape*) You got strong.

Jim They make us do sit-ups every morning. I could do hand-to-hand combat if I had to. I'm trained for it.

Else I wish someone would teach me. I had a dream the Germans came here at night and locked all the doors to the houses so we had to watch out the windows while they burned us down.

Jim That's stupid. That's a coward way to let yourself think.

Else Maybe I'm a coward.

Jim (*pulling her closer*) Then you'll need looking after.

Else What do we have here? Fishing boats? Farmers and shopkeepers . . .

Jim If they start something it won't be with this place.

Else Aren't you afraid?

Jim If they try they'll have the British navy in their way – one side of the Atlantic to the other –

Else You'll sew the ocean up, I suppose? With a needle and thread?

Jim Talking nonsense now. Talking kids' stuff . . .

Else No one says it out loud but everyone's scared here. I can taste it. I lie awake and I think about all the water all around us here and all the ways to go through it and over it.

Jim Talking loony again: that's you.

Else My cousin has a friend just come back from the fighting in Finland. He's organising, training people –

Jim He'll be training people for sitting on their arses.

Else What if he isn't? What if there was something for me to do. Something I *had* to do? What if I couldn't do it?

Jim I don't understand you.

Else You do. You know you do.

Jim If war starts it won't be you in it.

Else If war starts I'll never see you again.

Beat.

Will I?

Jim Do you want to get rid of me?

Else I shouldn't have written you letters. I shouldn't have done that.

Jim You pick a nice time to tell me.

Else I want to keep you, Jim.

Jim You can try.

He pulls her tightly to him.

Else How many hours left?

Jim Three. We'll hear the clock chime.

Else If you fall asleep I'll never forgive you.

SCENE FIVE: SECRETS

Kenny lies on his ship's bunk. Young Jim lies nearby, watching. The Band plays the sounds of the bunk room: creaking, rocking, sighing – a hummed melody emerging out of this. Perhaps the Band hangs in hammocks.

Kenny (*sung*)
    If there's a strong tide
    If there's a sharp wind
    If there's a hard fight
    If there's a tail spin
    We'll rise
    When time arrives
    Boys we'll rise.

The Band joins in the singing, harmonising.

Kenny / The Band (*sung*)
 If there's a war cry
 If there's a death knell
 If there's a fierce storm
 If there's a great swell
 We'll rise
 When time arrives
 Boys we'll rise.

 If there's a dark night
 If there's a blood moon
 If there's a last light
 Like an old tune
 We'll rise
 When time arrives
 Boys we'll rise.

Lights shift. Kenny and Jim sit tightly opposite each other, secretively sharing from a hip flask, their knees touching in the cramped space. They speak in low tones.

Kenny God, I need a fag.

Jim You had fags.

Kenny (*gesturing to the flask*) Swapped them for a nip, didn't I?

Jim
 Old rummy Ken was forever on the brink
 What he loved more than fags was the taste of the drink
 Fill him with smoke, soak him in rum
 Send him overboard with a kick up the bum.

Kenny You make that up?

Jim Just now.

Kenny It's fucking awful.

They laugh.

Jim How many hours now?

Kenny (*looking at his watch*) Three? Could be two. We'll be changing course soon. Heading inland.

Jim What's it gonna be like, you reckon?

Kenny What, Norway?

Jim Not Norway. I've been to Norway.

Kenny What you on about then?

Jim The fight. When we're in it.

Kenny Won't look like much from down in the wireless room.

Jim Not 'look like'. What'll it *be* like?

Kenny (*drinking*) What's Norway like then? Polar bears and that?

Jim No. Like Scotland only bigger. Sharper. Less pale.

Kenny You've never fucking been to Norway.

Jim I have!

Kenny There's no polar bears in Scotland.

Jim There aren't loads of polar bears in Norway: *bloody hell.*

Kenny You're all mouth you. I'm gonna call you Jimmy the Mouth –

Jim I bet you haven't even been to Morecambe Bay.

Kenny I saw three polar bears in Morecambe Bay and I'll fight any fella who says otherwise.

They laugh. They pass the drink.

Kenny It'll be quick I reckon. When it gets going. Like when we look back on it, it'll seem quick. But like a lot happened really quickly. It'll all be noise and banging heads. But we'll just be doing the job, like in training. We won't even be thinking.

Jim What if I start thinking?

Kenny What if you start writing a bloody poem?

Jim shoves him and he almost slips off his bunk. They laugh, drink again.

Jim Never been to Narvik. Never been up that far.

Kenny It'll be freezing. Mark my words. Icicle time. We'll be glad we're not on deck.

Jim We better hope we're not on deck.

Kenny If there's a reason for us to be on deck it's not the cold you'll be worried about.

Jim You don't think so?

Kenny I don't wanna think. That's the fucking rot.

Jim No harm in working something through –

Kenny
There was a young lad liked to work with his brain
He daydreamed his way in front a train
It took off his head, rolled him out flat
And the driver said: 'What d'you fucking think of that?'

Beat.

Eh?

Jim It's a bit graphic.

Kenny Better than you could bloody do.

They grin at each other.

Jim We should get some kip.

Kenny Not yet. Tell me something.

Jim Like what?

Kenny I don't know. None of the navy-boy bollocks you get with this lot. Something I can pin on you.

Jim What for?

Kenny For the purpose of general conversation. Jesus, who raised you?

Jim So you can take the piss out of me later?

Kenny So I can know you a bit. So when we sail this boat into a load of German gunners there's someone here I know just a little bit, alright?

Jim Alright.

Pause. Jim thinks.

I love to swim.

Kenny Bleeding hell . . .

Jim What?

Kenny This isn't a lonely hearts ad.

Jim I knew you were gonna take the piss.

Kenny I wanna know something *about* you. Something proper.

Jim What about you? What's proper about you?

Kenny All kinds.

Jim Go on then?

Kenny You know what an 'alias' is?

Jim Do I what?

Kenny Only back in Camden a fair few called me Vincent. Or round Camberwell I was Karlos. And in some crowds Stefano.

Jim Why?

Kenny I liked it. Putting on different names, different clothes . . . Everything's a game that way. Everything's a laugh.

Jim You're having me on?

Kenny That's something about me. And if you never get to learn anything else, if tomorrow morning's tipping over the edge, at least you'll know that one thing.

Jim Alright then.

Kenny And 'I love to swim' isn't anything. Everybody loves to swim –

Jim My dad taught me to swim. In the river and the canal. Took me to West Kirby beach once. Whips off his clothes, dashes off down the sand, diving in – daring me to follow him, to keep up. And I'm only about nine – swallowing water, panicking, but I'm damned if I'll let him see me scared. So I get me head down, kicking like a mad thing, going with the current, darting like a bloody pike. My dad's sticking his head above the water to cheer me on. (*Beat.*) By the time we looked round we were five miles down the coast at Heswall. Had to persuade the bus driver to take us home in just our undies.

Kenny You're messing about.

Jim He was sat there on the bus half naked, his hand in mine . . . beaming all over his bloody face.

Kenny Sounds like a good bloke.

Jim Wouldn't know.

Kenny How's that?

Jim Scarpered not long after. (*Beat.*) Got me up early one morning, made us both a cup of tea, told me to look after my mum, walked out the front door. Gone.

Kenny What did you do?

Jim What could I do? Watched him go.

Kenny 'Look after your mum'? *Christ . . .*

Jim Coward. Fucking *coward.*

Kenny
There was a young lad in his prime
Who could never make anything rhyme
With rhythm and metre he couldn't be neater
The rest: a complete waste of –

Jim Time?

Kenny Effort.

Jim (*grinning*) You're not funny.

Kenny Why you smiling then?

The boat judders, changing direction. They look up as the engine whirrs and grates.

SCENE SIX: BATTLE OF NARVIK / THE FOX

The sound of rushing water continues. Jim stands looking out. Else floats letters towards him. They disintegrate in the water.

Jim The *sound* of it . . . The bleeding *noise* . . . Buried in the belly of the boat – me and Kenny in the dark of the wireless room – heads down and voices coming in, Morse code tap-tapping: co-ordinates and sightings, all the wireless boys in all the boats of the convoy transmitting depths and distances. And we've got to listen, listen . . . Everything buried in static. We've got to listen while the engine clatters and hums, while the gunshot bounces off the mountains, while blasts of rock and wood and metal roll and roll somewhere above, while the hull scrapes through the channels – steel against stone. We've got to listen or else this boat's blind. This boat's blind and dumb in the mist of the Narvik fjord. Or else this boat's going down.

As he speaks Else pours ink into the water.

And when we hit . . . each time we get a hit . . . the cheers exploding from above . . . the yells and calls.

Else moves into his eyeline. He watches as she hops and dances about as in Scene Two. Perhaps he speaks over her singing.

Else (*sung*)
Where's your love, your only son?
He sleeps beneath the waves.
Where's your love, your only one?
His shining coat, his cap his gun.
Full fathom five, oh vow and sigh
You'll search the seas below
But where your love's gone, lonely one
No living soul can go.

Jim *I can see it.* I can see it so bright and sharp. When the guns stopped, in the hum after . . . Climbing out to the deck . . . The wreck of the deck . . . The open view of the mountains . . . Watching as the mist and smoke cleared . . . The bright white air and the bright white water . . . and all the way to the Narvik shore . . . the Jerry ships listing and rolling, sunk or sinking, scuttled or run aground, bomb-blasted and capsized. I saw a destroyer not half a mile away roll up on her beam ends

35

and disappear underwater like a trick – like nothing real. But there was something. There was something real . . . something so clear, so sharp. (*Beat.*) I knew what it was for. I knew what it meant.

Else 'I don't hear from you, Jim. I write and I write.'

Jim All of us on that ship, alive or dead . . . We'd offered ourselves up. We'd answered the call and we were victorious.

Else 'You've turned to smoke. Turned to air.'

Jim And there in the distance . . . a girl . . . a girl with long hair skiing down on to the shore . . . I watched her. And she was you, Else. In my mind she was you.

Else 'You've turned to silence. Turned to lies.'

Jim I wrote to you. I sent letters that couldn't reach you.

Else 'Perhaps you write and I don't receive them. Perhaps you won't read these words.'

Jim Letters burned by Germans, letters buried by snowdrifts and drowned in oceans.

Else 'But it's all the same, Jim. Whatever it is. It's all silence.'

Jim Why is it that you don't leave me, Else?

Else 'You ask such silly questions.'

Jim Does it have to be you?

Else 'They can't be the right questions.'

Jim I could remember my wife, my mother. Why must I have *you*?

Suddenly Else, Kenny and the Band all chant/sing quickly together.

Else / Kenny / The Band

The fox when he came to the farmer's gate,
Who should he see but the farmer's drake?
'I love you well for your master's sake
But I long to be picking your bone ee-oh.'
Bone-ee-oh, bone-ee-oh
'I long to be picking your bone-ee-oh.'

The farmer's wife she jumped out of bed,
Out of the window she poppe'd her head!
'Husband! Oh, husband! The geese are all dead,
The fox has been through the town, ee-oh!'
Town-ee-oh, town-ee-oh
'Husband! Oh, husband! The geese are all dead,
The fox has been through the town, ee-oh!'

Jim joins in, murmuring.

The farmer he loaded his pistol with lead,
Shot the old rogue of a fox through his head;
'Now,' said the farmer, 'I think you're quite dead;
Now I will bury your bone-ee-ohs.'
Bone-ee-ohs, bone-ee-ohs
'Now,' said the farmer, 'I think you're quite dead,
And no more you'll trouble the town, ee-oh.'

Lights down.

SCENE SEVEN: BOMBS ON LAMBETH

*The wireless room deep inside a ship. Static crackles,
Morse code taps through intermittently. Kenny wears
headphones, listening to incoming messages. Jim attempts
to tune a radio.*

Kenny North-westerly wind . . . in from Murmansk.
Speeds . . . 68.2 mph.

Jim makes a note of the weather front on a map.

Cold weather front through till morning. Minus 30 by 0400.

Jim notes this. Turning back to the radio.

Heavy snow and gales from inland. Plot a course north by north-east.

Jim marks this course on a map. Kenny squints, unable to hear the transmission – suddenly throws off his headphones.

Jim Something up?

Kenny Static up my earhole four hours straight, maybe I want a breather – that alright by you?

Jim No skin off my nose.

Kenny Sick of these dog watches. Four of these they've had me on this week.

Jim You'd rather be on deck hosing off the frozen vomit?

Kenny I'd rather be fucking *anywhere*.

Jim Yeah?

Kenny Yeah, and don't try being funny about it.

Jim Rather be under the arse of an elephant with diarrhoea?

Kenny Yeah, I would actually. Sounds nice.

Jim Rather be clinging to the bottom of the ship in your knack till your bollocks drop off?

Kenny Not using my bollocks for much anyway.

Jim Rather be in the First Officer's bed when he steams in drunk of a night?

Kenny You do my nut, you know that? You crack it right open.

Jim You're alright, Kenny. Course you bloody are.

Kenny You restoring my morale, Jim?

Jim You could have it worse.

Kenny pulls out a cigarette and attempts to light it, but can't get a flame.

Kenny Tell you what I can't stand: the post. All the fucking news. What good's news to me out here?

Jim You're complaining about getting letters?

Kenny So they're making more holes in London – can I lend them a bloody hand?

Jim My mam wrote – said half of Everton's rubble.

Kenny And does that help you sleep better? Knowing that?

Jim Is something up, Ken?

Kenny Not according to you.

Jim Bloody hell: the riddles. Nothing's straight with you.

Kenny Well, do you want me to be alright or not?

Jim I do *your* nut? You should try listening to yourself one time.

Kenny Give me a full night's sleep and my own pair of boots, I'll be sweetness and light.

Jim (*throwing him a lighter*) Shut up and have your cig.

Kenny Yeah, I'll have a cig. I'll have a drink, I'll do my watch, I'll sleep an hour, walk round in a circle and do it all again. I'll do a little dance shall I?

He starts to dance, stamping his feet ridiculously.

Jim This is what I'm talking about.

Kenny is still suddenly. He covers his eyes. Static from the radio, a faint voice. Jim tries to tune it in.

Jim Look busy, Ken. They'll be checking in on us.

Kenny They'll find me pinned to my post like Christ crucified. Where else am I gonna be?

Jim Shut up one second.

Two faint voices are talking to each other in Norwegian: a man and a woman, interrupted by static.

Kenny That German?

Jim No.

Kenny It's not from one of ours.

Jim Too faint . . . It's all broken up . . .

Male Voice (*on radio*) *Hvor er du?* . . .

Jim It's Norsk.

Kenny What?

Jim shushes him.

Two fishermen. Probably talking about the price of cod.

Female Voice (*on radio*) *Min elskede* . . .

Jim I don't think so.

Female Voice (*on radio*) *Min elskede* . . . *Min skatt* . . .

Kenny Fucking horrible language.

Jim signals for him to be quiet, fiddling with the dials, trying to get more clarity.

Female Voice (*on radio*) *Hvis du kunne komme tilbake til Bode* . . . (*Static.*)

Kenny What's she saying? Something dirty?

Jim They're up in the mountains.

Kenny They're idiots then.

Female Voice (*on radio*) *Hvis jeg kunne se deg . . .* (*Static.*)

Kenny If Jerry catches them they'll be eating bullets for breakfast.

   The voices are heard clearly suddenly.

Female Voice (*on radio*) *Hvis jeg kunne røre deg.*

Kenny What's she saying?

Male Voice (*on radio*) *Elske . . .*

Female Voice (*on radio*) *Jeg elske deg.*

Jim It's something private.

Kenny Well, pardon me.

   *They crouch, ears to the radio transmitter. The soft
   voices speak a poem.*

Female Voice (*on radio*) *Morgensolens glæde,
   o, du er min barndoms-tid*

Jim Something about time . . . Childhood.

Male Voice (*on radio*)
   *Mens du leger ren og hvid,
   Jeg kan næsten græde.*

Female Voice (*on radio*)
   *Aftensolens hvile,
   Ak, du er den vises ro –*

Male Voice (*on radio*)
   *Længer frem, så vil du jo
   Mod mit vindu smile?*

Jim They're talking about love.

The voices are lost in static again and gradually disappear. Static fades.

Kenny They blew up a factory in Lambeth. Munitions. Bombed it clean to pieces. Imagine that? Like a bucket of fireworks going off. The whole place blown a thousand ways. And all the people in it. My old man was in there they reckon. Not that they found anything of him.

Jim Who wrote you?

Kenny My mother. Fifteen bloody pages. Threw them in the water.

He laughs.

Jim I'm sorry, Kenny.

Kenny Me and all.

Jim No, I'm sorry – talking about an elephant's arse and all that.

Kenny hugs Jim very suddenly, tightly. Jim reciprocates. This lasts a moment too long. Kenny pulls away, turning back to the radio, checking his watch.

Nearly four o'clock. Who's betting they'll be late with the switch-over?

Kenny There'll be trouble with them gales.

Jim We'll steer it.

Kenny We'll have to bloody try.

He tries tuning in the radio, searching. The Band and Else move between the scattered objects tapping rhythms, humming. A song emerges. Kenny moves into shadow.

The Band (*sung*)
 If I had the word
 The whistle, the code
 Then I'd be a bird
 Or a whisper or both
 I'd be a fire
 A tower of smoke
 To my lost land I would roll, I would roll.

 If I could climb
 Where my heart strays
 I'd speak your words
 I'd follow your ways
 If I could sing
 All through your bones
 To my lost land I would go, I would go
 To my lost land I would echo, echo.

 Sid's voice is heard from the darkness, joining the
 singing. Jim listens, sinks to the ground.

The Band / Father (*sung*)
 If my hands were not stone
 And my feet not wood
 And my body not bound
 To the earth by blood
 I'd cut through the air
 Like a murder of crows.

 To my lost land I would go, I would go
 To my lost land I would echo echo.

SCENE EIGHT: FATHER'S VOICE

The last words of the song repeat as the Band move in
around Jim. He splutters, panicked, lifting his face for air.
Sid approaches.

Sid Calm now, come on, breathe. You can breathe.

Jim Dad?

Sid Just slow deep breaths.

Jim I . . .

Sid Don't panic – you'll make it worse.

Jim gasps, sobs, trying to catch his breath.

It's alright, kid. It's alright –

Jim I can't . . .

Sid How's this happened?

Jim It's not right.

Sid What isn't?

Jim They didn't have to shoot the fox.

Sid The fox?

Jim They didn't have to do that.

Sid The fox ate all the ducks.

Jim The fox loved the ducks.

Sid He ate all the ducks and geese. He picked their bones.

Jim What else could he eat? That's a fox's dinner. You said –

Sid It's only a story, Jimmy.

Jim They could've let him go or . . . sent him away.

Sid He would've come back. And he would've always been a fox. He'd 've done the same thing again.

Jim (*struggling again*) It wasn't his fault –

Sid Jimmy, calm. Breathe.

Jim breathes deeply, lets it out shakily.

Jim *They didn't have to kill the fox.*

Sid No. But they did kill it. And it was the right thing to do. So don't you worry about it any more, Jimmy. You hear me? (*Beat.*) *Jimmy?* Do you hear?

Jim Tell me a different story, Dad.

Sid It's too late, Jimmy.

Jim 'Bout the ships, 'bout the war.

Sid Aren't you sick of all them stories now?

Jim 'Bout the pirates – no, the mermaids.

Sid You're a bit too keen on them mermaids.

Jim You're standing on deck alone on watch –

Sid Alright, who's telling it?

Jim And it's pitch black night and you see a shape like the bow of a Prussian ship in the churning water –

Sid Only it's not a ship. It's the edge of a great big tail rising in the air and disappearing back under – then a huge head rears out of the mist – not ten feet away. A huge head of a giant fish with six yellow eyes and two hundred teeth like shining daggers. Now I stand firm, I don't flinch – I grab my rifle from the deck and I fire – but the monster raises a fin – flips the bullet away like a fly. And just then I get an idea – a strange and brilliant idea. I've heard it said that this part of the Arctic is populated by the most beautiful kind of mermaids – lonely girls flitting amongst the shingle, listening always for the singing of sailors. So I take a great deep breath, put on my best bass vibrato and I sing . . . (*Beat. He takes a breath as if about to sing.*) I won't do it for you now as it'd wake your mother, but rest assured it was the most wondrous and beauteous song anyone has ever sung – and as the last note lingered and the monster bore down to tear my head from neck, up from the waves rose a thousand shimmering maids, scales and skin silver and white in the moonlight, luminous hair streaming on the tide. They seized the beast by fin and tail, dug tooth and nail in its slimy flesh – threw a great silver rope between its jaws and dragged it under the waves like an enormous angry dog. And as the water began to calm, as the silence crept back in, one lone little red-haired maid flipped from the water and perched for a second beside me, placed a kiss on my cheek with her pretty pale lips and dived back in the deep with a twist of her tail.

Jim And what did it feel like when she kissed you?

Sid Wet and cold. Like a haddock.

Jim laughs.

Go to sleep now, Jimmy.

Jim Sing me the song. Sing like you sang to the mermaids.

Sid kisses him on the forehead.

Sid Go to sleep.

Jim takes Sid's hand, breathes deeply, steadily as if being carried away by waves. The Band breathes with Jim, propelling him from the floor as Sid moves away.

SCENE NINE: A CORPSE

Kenny and Jim huddle together on the freezing deck. They're on watch, trying to keep alert, keep warm.

Jim Jesus. Jesus.

Kenny What's he got to do with it?

Jim You'd think they'd bring us a bloody drink. Just a tot. At these bloody temperatures.

Kenny Just one? That do you?

Jim Or three. Or four.

Kenny They could bring us a four-course meal and all.

Jim laughs.

Is that funny?

Jim I don't know. I don't even know. (*Rubbing his hands for warmth.*) *Jesus.*

Kenny I told you: he's not listening.

Jim How much longer?

Kenny If you think I'm digging under my coat for the time –

Jim I reckon it can't be more than an hour.

Kenny Based on what?

Jim Intuition. The moon.

Kenny laughs.

What?

Kenny The moon? Who are you suddenly? Tonto?

Jim I've got an understanding of the night and its ways.

Kenny You've got nothing.

Jim Aren't you frozen, though? Tell me you're not frozen numb?

Kenny I'm grinning and bearing it, pal. That's how it's done.

Jim laughs.

Jim Go on – have another piss. See if it freezes this time.

Kenny We'll get home and tell them about our frozen piss and vomit, 'bout circling German subs the length of the fucking endless Arctic. They'll say 'Well done, son. You done your bit. Fancy a pint of mild?' They won't know anything about it.

Jim We could be telling it in German by then. Buying our beer with Reichsmarks.

Kenny You think that's funny, do you?

Jim I think everything's funny right now. (*Beat.*) And nothing. Nothing's funny.

Kenny (*pulling in closer to Jim*) Bloody hell it *is* nippy.

Jim Nippy?

Kenny (*sarcastic*) Chilly. You know? Not too mild. A little bit parky.

Jim (*sarcastic*) Cold enough to wear a coat.

Kenny I think my undies are frozen to my arse.

Jim laughs.

Might never get them off again.

Jim You don't think about it? If the Jerries pushed through? You don't think it could happen?

Kenny Nah. Not now we've got Russia.

Jim You sound like the bleeding wireless.

Kenny What do you want me to say?

Jim Doesn't seem real anyway. *After*. Not out here.

Kenny What you on about now?

Jim I think this is it. This is all we've got. The black night and the black sea. And the shining ice. I think it goes on forever.

Kenny Don't go actually loopy on me out here, Jim – I couldn't handle it.

Jim I think there could be anything on the other side. Or nothing.

Kenny I mean it, Jimmy: no fucking poetry.

Jim There could be sea monsters underneath us. Ready to turn us over.

Kenny That's your worry, is it?

Jim I just mean, right here, now. I could believe in anything. And nothing. In nothing ever after.

Kenny We'll go home. We will.

Jim What'll it look like?

Kenny Whatever it looks like. There'll be home. We'll get there.

Beat. Jim pulls tight to Kenny for warmth. Faint cries and distressed shouts in German are heard from below.

Jim (*listening*) That fucking Jerry again . . .

Kenny drops to his knees, banging on the deck.

Kenny (*shouting through the deck*) Button it, pal, or I'll button it for you.

Cries continue.

Jim All last night he was going for it.

Kenny Not one for suffering in silence, is he?

Jim Did you see when our lads pulled him out the water?

Kenny Spineless bastard.

Jim Shaking all over. Old fella too.

Kenny What about it?

Jim I don't know . . . I just keep thinking –

Kenny Here we go.

Jim Something about the way they were singing . . . The whole boat in flames and going under and the whole lot of them –

Kenny *Don't, Jim.*

Jim All of them voices in the dark –

Kenny Any bastard can sing, Jim.

Jim I know. I'm only saying –

Kenny And I'm saying *don't*. There's nothing in that. Nothing good. Nothing brave.

Jim holds his eye a moment.

What's up with you now?

Jim I can talk to you, Ken. You know what I mean? That's something. That means something.

Kenny pulls Jim closer and plants a kiss on him. A beat and Jim pulls back. He begins to laugh.

Kenny What's the joke?

Jim Us. *Jesus.* I miss women.

Kenny I don't.

Jim There was this girl in Oslo. When I was on the fishing boats before the war. She had this lovely way of making me feel stupid, this way of laughing at me so everything felt . . . easy. Safe. She was barmy like but *clever*. Sharp. We'd be up in this freezing little attic room she had –

Kenny Why you telling me this?

Jim I don't know. She was alright, you know? You'd 've liked her.

Kenny Sounds like a lot of people liked her.

Jim No, it wasn't like that –

Kenny Up in her room? What, straight off the boat and into her bed?

Jim She was brave like that. I know it sounds strange but –

Kenny I mean good on you, taking a ride on it and everything, but get wise, mate – don't start making it into a love story.

Jim You what?

Kenny All the lads do it. All the bastard time. Just 'cause we're out here. Just 'cause your scared.

Jim I'm not scared.

Kenny How many times did you meet this girl?

Jim Three times.

Kenny Three whole times in your whole bloody life. Three whole times three years ago?

Jim She's a girl I liked, alright? She came into my head.

Kenny I'm sorry if I'm breaking your heart –

Jim You're *not*.

Kenny Sorry to have to give it to you gently.

Jim Piss off, okay? She was just some bird.

Kenny Three years of the Norskies under occupation. She could be dead.

Jim Shut up.

Kenny You never think of that?

Jim Should never've said a word.

Kenny I'm only warning you, Jim. Don't hold her up like some kind of light.

Jim Wish I'd never bleeding spoken.

Kenny You don't know anything between then and now. You could be thinking about a corpse. A ghost.

Jim Tell me who you miss, Kenny.

Kenny What's that supposed to mean?

Jim You miss your old mum? You miss your sisters? Your mates? 'Cause you've never told me two things about them.

Kenny Just because I'm not Mummy's darling – writing every half-hour, telling her the colour of the sky –

Jim What do you know about it?

Kenny Ten letters back in every parcel: 'Are you a hero yet, Jim? Have you done me proud?'

Jim Shut up.

Kenny Don't think I don't read that shit. It gives me a good laugh after lights out.

Jim You know what I think, Kenny? I think it suits you being out here where nothing sticks. I think real life, real living back home, never went so well for you.

Kenny That your theory, is it?

Jim I think you made trouble for yourself. Probably more or less everywhere you went. I think you'd be happier lost at sea.

Kenny I keep myself vigilant. Exactly where I am. I keep my mind clean and focused in the here and now.

Jim And how is it you're gonna go home, Kenny? When you never write any letters back. When you don't keep pictures and you don't tell stories –

Kenny What the fuck's that got to do with it?

Jim Who are your sweethearts? Who are your friends?

Kenny They could all be dead, Jim – all my sweethearts and friends. Why do I wanna tell you their names? They could all be fucking smoke by the time I get to them.

Jim But that's the real world, Ken. That's all any of this is *for* –

Kenny This is *real*, Jimmy. This is about as real as it's ever gonna get.

    Beat.

Jim Then I'm sorry for you. I am.

    Kenny goes to reply but stops as the German sings suddenly from below deck: loud, strong, broken. They listen. Lights shift as the Band take over the singing, Else joining in: they are the crew of German sailors singing as the ship goes down.

Else / The Band (*sung*)
    Ob Sturm uns bedroht hoch vom Norden,
    Ob Heimweh im Herzen uns brennt;
    Wir sind Kameraden geworden,
    Und wenn es zur Hölle auch geht.

    Old Jim moves amongst the singers. They stare at him.

    Auf einem Seemannsgrab,
    Da blühen keine Rosen,
    Auf einem Seemannsgrab,

Da blüht kein Blümelein,
Der einz'ge Gruß, das sind die weißen Möwen
Und eine Träne die ein kleines Mädel weint.

The singers keep watching Jim, leaning in towards him.

SCENE TEN: ARCHANGEL

Jim stands facing out. All others watch Jim.

Jim Archangel . . . The frozen city glare. White buildings, white sky hitting me like a headache as I step on to deck, as we troop down the gangway. Spires and towers spiking the mist. Steam rising from my lips. As we move through the harbour . . . men in thousands. Uniforms, uniforms: blue, black and grey. Three destroyers in for re-fits and fellas are shifting cargo, crowding round trolleys and trucks, smoking and spitting, officers darting and yelling.

The cast sing in a brief harmonious burst: short fragments of 'Echo Song' overlapping eerily. Jim sways.

Someone's singing, but then there's always someone singing. At first when I hear it I don't think much. Then something familiar in the melody . . . And those words . . . Something in the gravel of the voice – the rise and fall . . .

Others sing: 'If I had the word . . . The whistle, the code', this looping, getting lost.

So before I can know it I feel it . . . Before I can see him I *know* . . . Before I find him I'm certain: there inside a knot of men, there not five foot away with all these fellas gathered round . . .

Others' sing: 'I'd be a bird. I'd be a bird.'

Singing . . . He's singing. Older, so much paler, greyer –

strange in his uniform but there, that voice – *his* voice, his eyes –

Others' sing: 'I'd be a fire, a tower of smoke.'

– on mine. His eyes flicker over me and land.

Others sing: 'Of smoke, of smoke . . .'

He smiles at first. Smiles through the song like he's seen an old friend, then something else . . . Something passes over him: a shadow or a cloud. His voice sticks as he stares at me, into me, stares with his mouth hung open and his lips turned pale. Like I'm the one surfacing out of the blue. Like I'm the one who's been a ghost all these years. And I swear every sound hangs in the air: just then, just for a broken moment – the ships, the crowd, the rush of the sea . . . Our breath held in our chests –

Singing cuts. Perhaps whistles are blown. Jim turns, twitches, looking around him.

Then 'Present, march! Forward, forward!' – orders called, bawled in chorus, whistles blown as half a thousand bodies ripple and shift, fall in line. The knot of men pulls loose and where is he, where he is . . .? Where in all these heaving currents? Hundreds of heads covered in caps, bobbing in time, streaming towards the water in different directions. I'm searching, circling, doubling back, busting through elbows and shoulders, pushing fellas down. Lieutenant's bellowing at me, 'Fall in line, Callaghan!' but I duck, dodge, stumble and there – there, trooping up on to a destroyer, laughing with the lad next to him, squinting against the sky, I shout, not a word but a sound – a holler – a cry – and he looks at me . . . Looks down to me, through me. He turns . . . climbs over the brow, ducks below decks and . . . gone. (*Beat.*) And I almost run after him. I imagine myself battering through the wall of men, scrambling up the gangway, finding him, pinning him, knocking him down, shouting: '*You saw me.* You bastard, you saw me. You saw me on the ice in Stanley Park when it started to crack and you told me to run. You saw me dancing with Mum that Christmas by the fire – when her hem caught light and you were laughing. You saw me on the front step counting birds: pigeon, sparrow, seagull – dust settling on your cup of tea. You saw me when I couldn't sleep and when I couldn't breathe . . . You saw me and you walked away.' You saw me and you *knew* me . . . and you walked away.

Lights down.

SCENE ELEVEN:
THE SINKING OF 'THE EDINBURGH'

Thick static. The wireless room of The Edinburgh. *Kenny listens to incoming Morse code, decoding and scribbling co-ordinates. Jim tries to tune in the radio, listening.*

Jim (*repeating the message*) Plotting a course south, south-westerly, 40 knots.

Kenny Why we going so fast?

Jim I don't bloody know.

Radio static: a mangled British voice. Jim tries to tune in.

Jim What's he bleeding saying?

Kenny We should've stayed with the convoy.

Jim The winds are too high – mangling the signal.

Kenny Shooting off on our own, it's fucking nuts.

The British voice comes in incomprehensible syllables, the tone urgent.

Jim (*still trying to tune the radio*) Whatever he's saying, he's not happy.

Kenny The stokers reckon we're carrying something.

Jim Carrying what?

Kenny They saw all these extra crates coming on. Some kind of precious cargo.

Jim Aren't we precious cargo?

Kenny Not likely.

Jim They're probably having you on. That's what this ship runs on: bullshit and rum.

Kenny You still in your sulk?

Jim I'm stating facts.

Kenny Ever since stop-over you've had your bottom lip stuck out.

Jim Why, you been watching me?

Kenny I've always got my eye on you, Jim. I'm your right-hand man.

Jim That right?

Kenny It is actually.

Jim Till the lads start taking the piss: then where are you?

Kenny You bolted across Archangel dock like a frightened horse. I can't help it if they think you're doo-dah.

Jim I went for a breather. I needed to breathe.

Kenny Don't worry about it, kid. They'll forget soon enough.

Jim Don't call me kid. I'm not a kid.

Kenny I didn't mean anything –

Jim You never do. That's your problem.

Kenny I haven't got a problem.

Jim Playing the wise old mate one minute, the nasty bastard the next –

Kenny The problem's all yours.

Jim You're one thing in the light, God knows what in the dark –

Kenny What you getting at?

Jim Who exactly are you, Ken? Or does it not matter? Is it all just a laugh?

Kenny Nothing's a laugh with you these days.

Jim 'Cause maybe it does matter actually. Maybe it matters to me.

The British voice on the radio again, incoherent, cutting in and out.

What's he telling us?

Kenny Hang on – someone's tapping through.

Morse code taps away. Sonar starts to bleep. Kenny listens.

There's something out there.

Jim (*turning sharply*) There's what?

Kenny (*listening*) U-boat sighted. Out from Murmansk. Radio through.

Beat. Jim stares at him. The Band turns to Jim suddenly whispering intensely: 'The stars they were shining and all things bright, The stars they were shining and all things bright . . .'

Radio the Captain. What's it gonna be?

Jim Ken?

Kenny (*reading the instruments*) Move, Jim.

Jim doesn't move. Sonar beeps get closer together. Whispers continue. Kenny jumps to his feet.

Reverse engines.

Jim only stares. Sonar beeps more intensely.

Tell 'em to reverse the engines.

He barges past Jim.

(*Into the radio.*) Reverse –

A massive explosion sounds, followed by intense high-pitched ringing. Else, Kenny and the Band are all thrown to the floor. They begin to beat their hands softly against the ground, slowly getting louder. Jim speaks facing out.

Jim Sirens. Face to the floor I hear feet beating through the walls, up through the decks above us. And I should move. I know I should move. Kenny's shouting something, grabbing my collar – dragging me up and out of the wireless room into the lightless corridor – into the press of men: my feet barely touching the floor as we shunt along in bursts. Someone cries out up ahead: 'Here! Here!' and I'm following the voice, finding the rung of a ladder, joining the queue of bodies climbing up, up through the hatches, through the decks towards the light. Fellas above me slipping, falling back – a boot hits my jaw and I barely feel it. And where's Kenny? And what's the damage? And what's the procedure? But up, up and out into . . . smoke . . . thick blackness. (*Beat.*) I'm squinting through stinging smog – looking towards the head of the ship and there's a crack – a great crack from stern to deck and light coming through. And all around me . . . we're in pieces: men without hands, without arms, men with faces doused in blood, men with blood where faces should be. (*Beat.*) Then 'Hatches! Lock the hatches!'

Somewhere in the smoke an officer's yelling: 'Lower decks flooding. Close the hatches.' And I can't move for fear, but there's lads shouting 'Aye' and 'Aye sir', 'Aye sir' and all along the deck the hatches are clanging shut, the valves are straining tight, sealing off all beneath, as I picture them . . . the dozens of men trapped below . . . lifting their chins as the ice water rises, gasping as it covers them. And then I hear it . . . Coming up through the floor, up through my bones . . . The knocking. The clanging and scraping at the pipes . . . all the drowning men begging to be let out, begging for their lives. (*Beat.*) That endless clatter on and on. That endless angry protest of the dead.

Kenny, Else, the Band all bang on the floor with more intensity, rising slowly so their eyes are locked on Jim.

SCENE TWELVE: MURMANSK

The banging changes rhythm until it is the beat of the traditional Russian song 'Katjuscha', played fast and wild. We're in a makeshift bar in a camp in Murmansk.

The Band (*sung*)
  Rastsvetali iabloni i grushi,
  Poplyli tumany nad rekoj.
  Vykhodila na bereg Katjuscha
  Na vysokij bereg na krutoj
    (*Repeat last two lines.*)

  La la lah . . . (*Etc.*)

  Sing a song for pretty Katjuscha
  Sing a song for an ordinary girl
  While he walks a faraway border
  In her heart their love she will preserve
    (*Repeat last two lines.*)

  Hey, hey . . . (*Etc.*)

Jim begins to stamp around, dancing badly, very drunk. He drags Else up to join him except it isn't Else, it's a Russian woman: Lucya. Kenny watches, drinking. The Band finishes and the others applaud. Lucya leans on Jim's shoulder. He staggers slightly. The Band takes up a soft, slow, meandering version of 'Where's Your Love?'

Jim You look so much like . . . It's mad. I thought it before . . . but now looking at you . . . You look *just* like her.

Lucya (*in Russian*) No more dancing? You've had too much?

Jim You're older. But no, she'd be older now . . . Not that I'm saying you look old or –

Lucya (*in Russian*) You're flattering me. Or you're trying to.

Jim You know what I'm saying, don't you? You know enough. You understand?

Lucya (*in Russian*) Will you find me a drink? I doubt you're good for anything else.

Jim And I know enough what you're saying. I mean I don't know a word but . . . it's enough. It's like I know you. You look *so* much like her.

Lucya (*in Russian*) Look at you: just a boy searching for your sweetheart . . .

Jim 'Cause it's queer isn't it? We're only just not enemies. Few months gone you'd 've spat at me sooner than danced with me. Eh, Russki? We'd have been fighting with pistols.

Lucya (*in Russian*) What do you call me?

Jim You get what I'm saying? A few months back? (*Lifting his hand to her head like a gun.*) Bang bang.

Lucya (*in Russian, turning away sharply*) What does this mean?

Jim (*stumbling after*) Don't. No, don't, it's not like . . . (*Catching her arm.*) I'm glad I . . . We can talk now. We can know each other.

Lucya (*in Russian, pulling away*) I wanted to dance, that's all.

Jim 'Ere listen, listen –

He makes a grab for her again and she pulls away, frightened.

Kenny (*calling over*) Why don't you leave the girl alone, Jim?

Jim (*to Lucya*) Hey, hey, calm. What's happened?

Kenny She doesn't want you hanging off her like a bad shirt.

Jim (*taking hold of her arms*) Hey, shush . . .

Lucya (*in Russian, struggling*) Let go of me, yes?

Kenny (*approaching*) Jim, get your fucking hands off her.

Jim (*hands in the air*) My hands aren't on her. I'm tryna' talk to her.

Kenny She's terrified.

Jim She's fine. (*To Lucya, loudly.*) Aren't you? Tell him. (*Gesturing.*) You're okay.

Lucya (*in Russian*) You British are all madmen. Bullies and madmen.

Kenny Don't worry, darling, the kid talks big but he's nothing to bother about.

Lucya moves away quickly.

Jim What are you calling me? (*Looking around for Lucya.*) Look at that! I was on to something there.

Kenny You'd only give way under pressure, Jim. When it counts, you know what I mean?

Jim I liked her. Does that bother you?

Kenny You bother me. You and your talk and your nothing fucking else.

Jim I'll talk to who I want.

Kenny You'll talk the ocean dry but there'll be nothing *to you*, Jim.

Jim Say what you're saying for once in your bloody life.

Kenny I'm saying you're gutless. I'm saying you're gutless to the point of bleeding danger. I'm saying we might've had some chance against that U-boat if you hadn't frozen at your fucking post.

Jim spits in his face. Kenny barely flinches.

Kenny You gonna try and deny it, Jim?

Jim There was no chance.

Kenny Seventy-eight dead . . .

Jim We never had a chance.

Kenny You're two men, Jim: the man you think you are and the man you are when it matters. You're no man at all.

Jim You really wanna talk to me about who's the man here?

Kenny I think I just did.

Jim You want that do you? 'Cause, bloody hell, it's a risk you're taking.

Kenny What is it you think you've *got*, Callaghan?

Jim I think I've got you pinned. From the inside out.

Kenny I think you're drunk. And ashamed of yourself. And so does everyone else here.

Jim Why don't you talk to the girls, Ken? Why don't you bother some skirt some time?

Kenny Shut up.

Jim (*staggering towards him*) What you are . . . What *you* are . . .

Kenny I'm warning you, Jimmy –

Jim And you say *I'm* not a man?

Kenny runs at him suddenly, laying a rough punch, knocking him to the ground. Jim overpowers him, getting a grip round his neck. Kenny splutters and gags. A beat and Jim releases him. He stares at Kenny.

(*Quietly.*) There was no chance. Say it.

Kenny Seventy-eight men.

Jim We had no chance.

Kenny Seventy-eight of us.

Jim We had no chance. *Say it.*

Kenny stares at him, grins coldly. A beat and then Jim shoves him away, moving to leave.

Kenny There goes Jimmy the Mouth. He talked so much manure he sprouted daisies.

Jim (*turning*) It's not *funny*, Kenny.

Kenny There goes Mouth Jim. Watch out, ladies . . . he'll break your *fucking* heart.

Beat. Jim stalks away. Lights dim on Kenny as the Band play the tune to 'Take My Heart'. Jim stumbles, stares out. Lights shift around him.

Jim Out in the frozen night . . . the cold sinking through my shirt and into the skin . . . softly, gently. The sounds of the bar swinging in the air. (*Beat.*) And if I could stop . . . If I could reach back and hold time still. If I could turn back, go back. If I could drag him up and take his hand and laugh with him a last time . . . (*Beat.*) But on, on . . . stumbling, staggering out into the wide white wastes of Murmansk . . . my chest warm with liquor and hate and shame. Down to the shore and the thick churning ocean: the black and endless water out to the black and moonless sky. And if I was to swim . . . If I was to throw myself beneath that tide . . . If I was to let the water take me, till the cold felt like heat, like love . . .

The Band hum, harmonising high-pitched.

Then far, far out, pinpointing the horizon . . . lights, lamps of ships . . . dozens of them pulsing and blinking, growing and fading like stars turning across centuries.

The Band, Else and Kenny begin to flash lights in the dark in a sporadic rhythm.

Navy ships and cargo ships and fishing boats and mad Russians on adventures . . . all talking to me. All dancing with their code. Marking it like a constellation. And I read your name there . . . Else. Else. Else. I read it over and again. And it's enough. It's promise enough.

He remains still, looking up and out as the Band sings.

The Band (*sung*)
　　How much love to kill a heart
　　How much love to keep it beating
　　How many hours to mend the pieces
　　How many words
　　Always repeating?

Take my heart in your hands
Take my heart in your hands

How much wine in the water
How much blood on the ground
How much joy and how much slaughter
How many swim
How many drown?

Take my heart in your hands
Take my heart in your hands
Mend it with glue, mend it with sand
Mend it with lies and reprimands
But take my heart
Take my heart.

*The last line is repeated. Lights continue to flash,
gradually slowing and stopping.*

SCENE THIRTEEN: OSLO, MAY 1945

*The attic room. Jim is pointing a gun at Else. She stares
at him. He stares back.*

Else What is it you want to do?

Jim You think it's up to me?

Else Is it not? Is it not up to anyone?

Jim Stop talking, stop talking.

Else Are we not people now, only flags and orders?

Jim What do you know about it?

Else You tell me what you want to do.

Jim I wish I'd never found you. I wish I'd never tried.

Else What is it you think I deserve?

Jim I don't want to think about you, Else. I thought about you for five years – I was thinking about someone else.

Else What else was I supposed to do?

Jim *Supposed to do?*

Else He chose me. From the first day they landed here –

Jim I don't want to know.

Else – he had his eyes on me, following me around . . .

Jim *I don't want to hear your love story.*

Else He did love me actually. He did love me.

Jim You nasty little . . . you . . .

Else He loved me and your people shot him through the head and I watched them. So no, I'm not who I was. I'm not who you thought of. And what choice did I have in that?

Jim We made choices. Then you made other choices.

Else There's a camp outside the town . . . where they took rebels – tortured them, half starved them. He protected me from that.

Jim You sold yourself, Else – call it any old thing you like –

Else They were murdering people in the streets –

Jim Sorry to hear you had a tough old war. As for me, it's been a walk in the park.

Else What was I supposed to do?

Jim You were supposed to die.

Beat.

Anything rather than *that*.

Else Aren't I going to die now? Aren't you going to kill me, Jim? Isn't it the same one way or another?

Pause.

Jim He didn't love you.

Else He loved me. And I loved him. In the end. He was doing what he had to, like I had to, like you –

Jim Not like me. Not a bit like me.

Else He'd have sooner there'd never been a war but as there was –

Jim Shit. Nasty, dirty shit.

Else You never used to swear.

Jim You never used to fuck Jerries.

Pause.

Else Do it, Jim . . . I'd rather *you* did it . . . The Norwegian women who lived with the officers – the beautiful girls with their blonde hair in rolls. They stripped them naked in the street. Half drowned them and whipped them and hung them from the railings.

Jim I carried your picture. I kept you alive . . . I said your name, I . . . You didn't love him.

Else I did. So shoot me.

Beat.

Jim I was looking for you . . . Coming into Oslo my boat was at the front of the flotilla and the people were rowing out and crying and cheering and lifting up their hands for bread. And we threw it down to them like confetti. And I as looking for you in amongst them. And then in the street, in the crowds. I was going to take you in my arms and kiss you. Except you weren't there, you were here, you were hiding beneath the floorboards in the room where I left you. Crouched like a rat.

Else I'll lie down on the bed. It'll be done so fast.

Jim I saw your mother and asked for you, she spat on the ground.

Else It should be you. I want it to be you.

Jim (*turning away*) Get out. Just get out.

Else *Please*, Jim –

Jim Get away from me.

Else You can't know what it was. You can't ever know that.

Jim I know what you are: I know you're a whore, I know you're a liar, a traitor –

Else I'm none of those things.

Jim You are what you *do*, Else. It's all any of us are. It's all we've *got*.

Else Have you ever seen a person torn apart by a crowd, Jim?

Jim Don't talk to me about what I've seen –

Else You know what that looks like up close?

Jim It's not what I've seen, it's what I can't stop seeing.

Else Then show some *mercy*.

Jim You think there's mercy where I've been? Lads blown to bits, to dust, lost in sand and ice and water, and not because they were heroes or cowards or anything else –

Else I lost people too.

Jim You don't know what it *means*. Mate I had – best mate I *ever* had – got posted to a destroyer, hit a Jerry mine. He burned alive below decks. That's what they said. I never saw it but it's *here*. (*Tapping his head.*) I'm living it, Else. I'm *in it*. I *am* it. And you think *you* deserve *mercy*?

Else Do it. Shoot me.

He approaches her slowly, raises the gun to her head to shoot. He watches her a moment, lowers the gun. She stands staring, gasping.

Jim Go outside, Else. Run through the streets. Run out into the crowds and see how far you get.

The Band plays an eerie instrumental reprise of 'Where's Your Love?'

SCENE FOURTEEN: THE PARADE

The instrumental continues: a strange, distorted version.

Jim We're marching through the streets. We're parading ourselves and the sky's full of Norwegian flags – blue and red. Every last Jerry soldier and SS bastard driven out, caught out, killed or transported – and we the liberators . . . we the battered and bruised boys of the British navy – drunk on victory and relief and a dozen bright and sleepless nights. Hundreds of us. Thousands in convoy across the square . . . The army boys up ahead and the people running out to holler and dance – grabbing at our clothes as we pass. As if touching us is touching freedom. Touching the solid truth of it. We're marching into the clear blue day and that's when I see her.

The Band pick out shimmering percussion as Else and Kenny rise up from the ground.

I see her hanging from the railings of the palace. She's battered and bloody but it's her face – I can see her face, her hair dripping wet. Her head's back and her mouth's open and right through her throat – the spike of the railing sticks right through her throat . . .

Else and Kenny dance, pulling together and apart, twisting and turning in the water.

And she's gone. I'm marching and she's gone and on and on and how to stop? And the flags and the shouting and the clear blue morning sky – the ice air cutting my breath. And over and over in my mind: her battered body, her beautiful body, Else with the German, Else with me. Her and him and me and her. Twisting and turning in that bed in that little attic room. And she said she loved me and she said she loved him. And she said he loved her. And we are all but beating hearts. We are guts and blood and animal things. And where are the lights? And where are the lights?

Else and Kenny spin faster. They're falling, they're drowning.

On and on and faster now. The tall white buildings and the flags flailing from open windows. Some of our lads are singing. They're singing a dirty song, a cheerful old dirty song. And I remember Narvik. I remember the morning we blasted those Jerry ships to pieces in the mist of the Narvik fjord. And we danced and drank and bellowed songs after: our hearts so full and so loud and we were all the world and the only human animals in it.

And for that moment . . . for that moment it was true. We were true. (*Beat.*) Then 'Monsters!' Someone's shouting it. Two old men are being dragged down the street – rope round their feet and hands. They're stumbling and falling. Women spitting on them and throwing stones shouting: 'Traitors!' 'Quislings!' 'Pigs!' And I can't feel my body suddenly. And I'm reeling forward and my feet go from under me and my face hits the gravel.

Jim reaches out his hand towards Else, straining.

And in the black I see Else twisting and turning in the water: her hair billowing white around her; her feet and hands bound. And I'm reaching for her, I'm reaching for her . . . And if I could just . . . If I wasn't so . . . If I could just . . . if I could just . . .

Else and Kenny take hold of Jim, lowering him slowly to the ground. Jim struggles again and again. The Band hums as they circle, moving in. Else and Kenny each take one of Jim's hands. He closes his eyes as the sound of water becomes overwhelming. Lights close in on him. Sudden knocking from above: someone banging at the door. Lights shift as other sounds stop abruptly, the ghosts recoiling. Jim opens his eyes. Knocking gets louder.

I'm here. (*Beat. Louder.*) I'm here.

Lights down.

End.